CREEPY CREATURES

CREEPY CREATURES

Emily Ann Davison

Collins

Contents

Chapter 1 Looks like a vampire! 7

Bonus Vlad Drakulya: the inspiration
   for Dracula............................. 20

Chapter 2 Feeds like a vampire 23

Bonus Bats vs penguins 36

Chapter 3 Acting like a zombie 39

Chapter 4 Mind control parasites 55

Bonus Classified: new discovery 68

Chapter 5 Ghost creatures 71

Bonus More creepy creatures 84

Chapter 6 Newly discovered
   ghost creatures 87

Bonus Creatures of the deep 102

Glossary 104

About the author 106

Book chat 108

CHAPTER 1
Looks like a vampire!

What do vampire squids and vampire squirrels have in common? Apart from their name, they both remind us of vampires by how they look. But what *are* vampires?

When you hear the word 'vampire', what do you think about? A creature with fangs and glowing eyes, that drinks blood? Do you imagine vampires wearing capes? Are the vampires in your imagination **nocturnal**? Do they sleep in a coffin? Can they transform into a bat? These are all features of how we imagine vampires today. We know that vampires aren't real (phew!), but where did the idea of these creatures come from?

The word 'vampire' wasn't used until nearly 300 years ago!

At that time, many people in Eastern Europe were dying and no one knew the cause. Locals wrongly accused some of the people who had recently died in their villages of being vampires. They thought these people were coming back to life as vampires and killing more people.

False rumours spread and the terrified villagers started to dig up the graves of suspected vampires. They would drive a stake (a sharp wooden stick) through the heart of the dead body, because they thought this would stop these suspected vampires from killing more people.

But it was the books written by Emily Gerard that brought the myths from Transylvania, Eastern Europe to the UK. During her travels, Emily collected stories from local people. Many of these stories included the nosferatu, or vampire. Her research inspired the idea for one of the most famous vampires of all time – Count Dracula!

Bram Stoker's book *Dracula* was published in 1897. He invented the idea that vampires could transform into bats. People still enjoy reading his book today.

Since 1897, there have been many books, television programmes and films that feature vampires, and plenty of film adaptations of Bram Stoker's *Dracula*.

But vampires aren't always scary. In the *Hotel Transylvania* films, Dracula has created a resort for monsters to protect them from humans. And the Count von Count in *Sesame Street* is famous for entertaining young children and teaching them to count.

Many vampires in popular culture have fangs, hunt at night, wear a cape and, of course, they suck blood. The creatures we're going to find out about have some of these characteristics, too.

Even though vampires are not real, vampire squids and vampire squirrels most definitely are!

Vampire squids

Name: *vampire squid*

Area of the world: *all over the world, in tropical waters*

Habitat: *the shadow zone of the ocean (technically called the oxygen minimum zone), depths of 600—900 metres*

Appearance:
- *about the length of a ten-year old's arm!*
- *webbing between their eight arms*
- *red and black body*
- *big blue eyes*

Vampire squids belong to the same class of animal as squids – both are cephalopods. However, despite their name, vampire squids are neither vampires nor squids!

Vampire squids were discovered over a century ago, a few years after Bram Stoker's *Dracula* was published. When a new animal is discovered, scientists give it a scientific name. The scientific name of the vampire squid is *Vampyroteuthis infernalis*, which means 'vampire squid from hell'!

They were given this name because the webbing between vampire squids' arms is dark red and looks like a vampire's cloak. However, unlike vampires in folklore, vampire squids are gentle sea creatures.

FACT: *Vampire squids have been around since before the dinosaurs! They are a 'living fossil' because they have hardly changed over millions of years.*

Vampire squids live in the shadow zone of the ocean. At this depth it is completely dark. Of all the creatures on our planet, they have the biggest eyes in comparison to their size – this helps them see better in the intense darkness of the deep sea.

For many years, scientists thought that vampire squids were like octopuses, waiting in the dark to feed on live prey. In 2012, scientists finally discovered what they feed on. Vampire squids don't feed on blood like vampires, and neither do they feed on live prey. Instead, they feed on marine snow. This is ocean debris that has fallen into the depths of the ocean and includes algae, dead fish and the snot from tiny sea creatures called larvaceans. Vampire squids have two long **filaments** covered in tiny hairs. They use these to gather up the food and roll it into **mucus** balls.

When vampire squids feel threatened, they pull their arms over their head and turn their webbing inside out. This reveals rows of spines. Their arms are covered in spots which produce light. Vampire squids can flash in the dark water. They may do this to startle and confuse predators, so the vampire squids can escape.

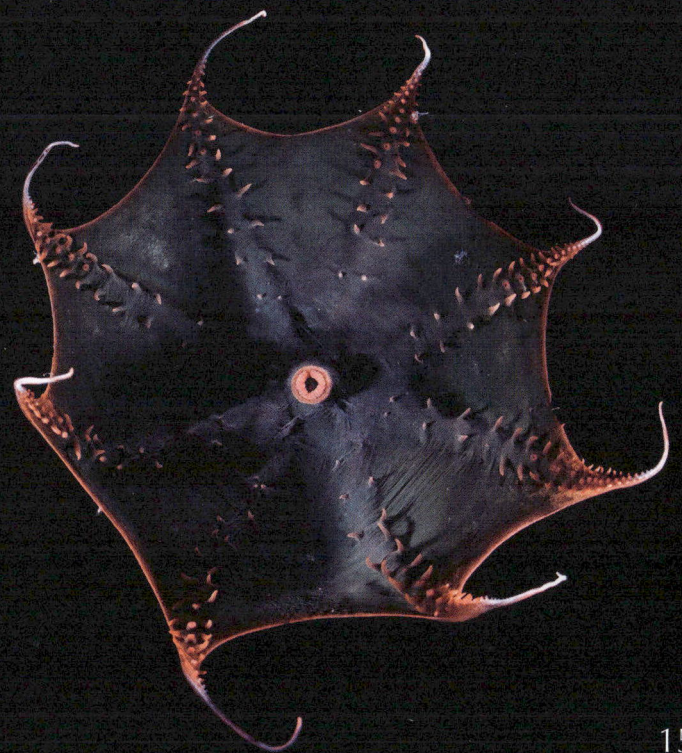

Vampire squirrels

Name: Bornean tufted ground squirrel

Nickname: vampire squirrel

Area of the world: Borneo

Habitat: lower branches of trees in rainforests

Appearance:
- larger than a tree squirrel
- large, sharp teeth on top and bottom jaw
- reddy brown fur
- long, bulky bushy tail

Vampire squirrels are a type of ground squirrel, but what does this mean? In the squirrel family, there are tree squirrels and ground squirrels. Tree squirrels, as the name suggests, live in the trees. Ground squirrels, on the other hand, live on the ground or in burrows.

Bornean tufted ground squirrels have been nicknamed vampire squirrels, due to their sharp teeth.

The Dayak people who live and hunt in the Borneo forests believe that the squirrels leap from treetops onto the deer and attack them. This belief may have come about because the hunters in the area sometimes found dead deer that had been partially eaten, and they blamed the squirrels for their deaths. However, in 2020, researchers discovered the squirrels eat extremely hard seeds and that's why they have sharp teeth – to break into them! They don't actually attack deer.

The squirrels have enormous bushy tails. In fact, they have larger tails, in comparison with their body, than any other mammal! The reason for these massive tails is unknown, but it might be to help protect them from predators.

FACT: *These squirrels are elusive which has made them difficult for scientists to study. It wasn't until 2015 that vampire squirrels were first caught on camera!*

Dayak people

Borneo

Bonus
VLAD DRAKULYA:
THE INSPIRATION FOR DRACULA

Vlad Drakulya, otherwise known as Vlad the Impaler, was a Romanian ruler from the mid-1400s.

He was famous for his cruelty and used stakes to stab (or impale) his enemies. Vlad Drakulya was one of the inspirations for Bram Stoker's novel *Dracula*.

Apparently, Vlad Drakulya once stayed in Bran Castle in Transylvania. Today, many people call this 'Dracula's Castle'. It's true that in Bram Stoker's novel, Count Dracula lived in a castle in Transylvania. But Bram Stoker never visited Bran Castle, and he didn't base the castle in his book on it. However, that hasn't stopped people flocking to visit 'Dracula's Castle'!

CHAPTER 2
Feeds like a vampire

We've previously looked at creatures which LOOK like a vampire, but what about creatures that FEED like one?

The idea of bloodsucking creatures has been around in folklore for hundreds of years. As with many stories and legends, there are variations as the stories have been passed down over time.

The stories found in Greek mythology are over 2,000 years old. They tell of many different gods, goddesses and creatures, including a phantom called Empusa. Some stories say that Empusa drank the blood of sleeping men!

There is a similar creature found in Scottish mythology. In these myths, the Baobhan Sith took the form of a beautiful woman who attacked men and drank their blood.

Another bloodthirsty creature from folk tales is the Strigoi from Romania. In these Romanian stories, the Strigoi are spirits who drink milk, but when their supply runs out, they drink blood instead.

In First Nation Australian mythology, there is the Yara-Ma-Yha-Who. This red frog-like creature waits in trees, for travellers who stop beneath them. The creature climbs down and drinks their blood using suckers on the end of its arms and legs.

Next, the Yara-Ma-Yha-Who eats the traveller whole, then spits them back out. The person will be unharmed but will be left with a reddish tint on their skin!

In China, there are legends about the Jiangshi, a type of undead creature. The legends say these creatures rest during the day, and at night, they hop about with their arms outstretched. Some stories say they kill people by absorbing their life source.

These are just some of the legends of bloodsucking creatures, and creatures of the undead, from across the world. But these are just stories, right? There aren't really creatures that feed off blood – or are there?

Vampire bats

Name: common vampire bat

Area of the world: Mexico, Central America, South America

Habitat: completely dark places, such as the roofs of caves, abandoned buildings or the hollows of trees

Appearance:
- *their body is nine centimetres long (similar to an adult's thumb)*
- *wingspan 18 centimetres*
- *brown, grey or orange fur*
- *tailless*
- *sharp teeth*

Bats are quite special. They're the only mammals that can fly. However, vampire bats are even more unique – they are the only mammals that feed entirely on blood!

Most bats are nocturnal and this includes vampire bats. During the day, they sleep hanging upside down. These bats live in large groups called colonies, typically in the hundreds.

Vampire bats only start to hunt when it's completely dark. They swoop and land near their prey and creep towards them. Unlike other bats, they can run and hop on all four legs.

Vampire bats typically feed on the blood of cows and horses, but they have sometimes bitten humans. (This is rare, so don't panic!) They don't kill their prey. Sometimes, the prey don't even realise a vampire bat is feeding from them! The bites can cause infections, though, or carry diseases.

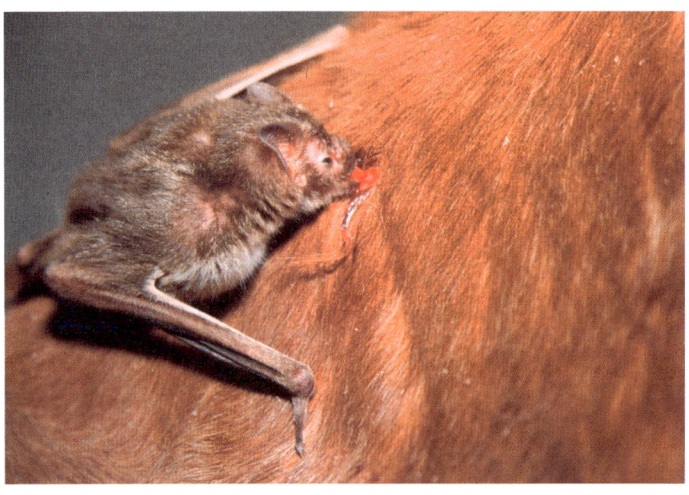

Vampire bats don't have many teeth, as they feed on liquid, so they don't need teeth for chewing. However, the few teeth they have are very sharp, so they can pierce their prey's skin.

Vampire bats also have heat sensors on their noses which helps them detect the warm blood flowing through their prey's veins. That's how they know where to bite them. They lap up the flowing blood with their tongues. Their saliva stops the blood from **clotting**. This keeps the blood flowing from the small wounds, to make sure the bats have plenty to drink.

It's only recently that researchers have discovered how adult vampire bats survive on blood alone. In their gut, they have special bacteria which help them digest it.

FACT: Vampire bats can locate their prey by the sound of its breathing.

Unlike the vampires in folk tales, which are **immortal**, vampire bats can only survive two days without drinking blood, otherwise they will starve. However, scientists have discovered that the bats help one another. Vampire bats make friends by grooming each other. Once these friendships form, if one bat hasn't fed enough during a night, another vampire bat will share their meal. They **regurgitate** blood they've drunk, to feed the other bat.

Vampire finches

Name: *vampire ground finch*

Area of the world: *Wolf Island and Darwin Island in the Galápagos*

Habitat: deciduous *forests and shrubland*

Appearance:
- *pointy beaks (adapted for skin piercing)*
- *males are black*
- *females are grey*

Before looking at how vampire finches got their name, there's another extraordinary thing you should know about these birds.

Charles Darwin was a well-known English scientist who studied the natural world. In the 1830s, he visited the Galápagos Islands. While he was there, he observed that the different species of finches all had unique beaks and behaviours. One of these birds was later called the vampire finch. All of these different finches are often referred to as Darwin's finches and his observations helped him develop his theory of **evolution**! *Darwin is famous for writing about this theory in his book* On the Origin of Species.

Vampire finches are different to the other finches on the Galápagos Islands. The clue is in their name! They land on other, bigger birds and peck into their skin at the base of the bigger birds' feathers. Then they lick up the blood that comes out. Surprisingly, these bigger birds are not badly affected by having their blood taken. In fact, they don't seem irritated by vampire finches pecking at them and they stay still while it happens. If it does bother them too much, they will just fly away.

Blood is only one part of the vampire finches' diet. They also feed on seeds, nectar, insects and eggs. So, why do they need to drink blood as well? Scientists think that the finches turn to pecking larger birds and drinking their blood during times when their normal food sources are scarce. The blood has some nutrients in it, so it helps them to survive until they're able to return to their normal food.

> **FACT:** *The Galápagos Islands have other vampires too! Avian vampire flies feed on finch chicks, including vampire finch chicks. The flies lay their eggs in the nests and the **larvae** feed on the chicks' blood.*

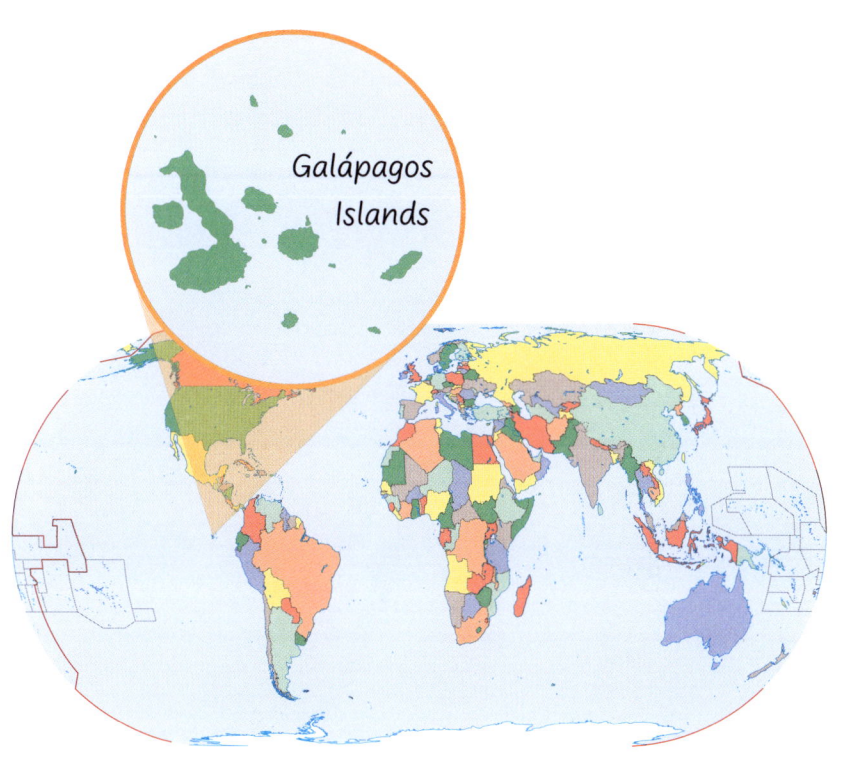

Bonus
BATS VS PENGUINS

In Southern Peru, vampire bats normally feed off sea lions. However, sometimes they attack Humboldt penguin chicks.

Being young, the chicks are vulnerable and unaware of the danger of vampire bats.

Thankfully, adult Humboldt penguins don't just stand by!

They scare the bats off by being extremely loud and kicking dirt at them. Not only that, they also use their poo as a weapon. They squirt it at the bats, to shoo them away!

CHAPTER 3
Acting like a zombie

Some creatures are called 'zombie creatures' because they can start to act like zombies when they're infected by certain diseases. But what do we mean by zombies?

Zombies are the walking dead! If zombies were real, how would you recognise one? Here are some key zombie characteristics:

- human-looking
- arms stretched out in front (don't mistake this for somebody exercising!)
- vacant look (a bit like some people when they've just woken up!)
- rotting flesh – stinky!
- super strength
- silent.

Where does the idea of zombies come from?

Zombie stories seem to have started about 200 years ago, in Haiti. The legends state that sorcerers used magic to reanimate dead people, raising them from the grave as zombies. These zombies had no free will. They were entirely under the control of the sorcerer.

In 1929, William Seabrook published his novel *The Magic Island* about somebody travelling to Haiti and witnessing the dead rising again as zombies. This is when the word 'zombie' first became well-known.

In more modern stories, zombies come about in different ways. In some stories, the zombies come alive when **parasites** or viruses take control of a dead body and turn it into the 'walking dead'. Sometimes in these stories, a zombie can bite a human and transform them into a zombie too!

Today, many popular ideas about zombies come from a scary film called *Night of the Living Dead*. Since that film was released around 60 years ago, zombies have found their way into cartoons, films, books and games. Zombies feature in the famous children's book series *Goosebumps*. They also appear on many television programmes and films including *Monster High* and *Hotel Transylvania*.

There are some real-life creatures that develop zombie-like behaviours.

Zombie sea stars

Name: sunflower sea star

Area of the world: Northeast Pacific and the region from Alaska to Southern California

Habitat: different habitats including **rocky reefs** and **kelp forests**

Appearance:
- can grow up to one metre
- weigh about five kilograms (the weight of an adult cat)
- colour ranges from bright orange and yellowy red to brown
- the adults can grow up to 24 arms!

Before delving deep into some gruesome facts about zombie sea stars, it is important to understand what sea stars actually are.

Sea stars were previously known as starfish. This name is no longer used, because it was misleading. These animals are not a type of fish at all! They don't have gills or fins, and they only live in saltwater. This is why they were renamed sea stars.

But what about zombie sea stars? Well, we call zombies 'the living dead' because their bodies decay and parts separate. Sunflower sea stars have earned their nickname 'zombie sea stars' because of this zombie characteristic.

In 2013, sunflower sea stars were seen pulling off their own arms! What was even creepier was that the arms crawled away from their body, all on their own!

Scientists have since discovered that a disease called 'Sea Star Associated Densovirus' (SsaDV) had infected these unfortunate creatures. This disease can affect not only sunflower sea stars, but up to 20 other species of sea stars too.

A team of scientists have wondered if the disease is linked to climate change as they have discovered a connection between an increase in the disease and the warmer temperature of the ocean.

Sadly, this disease brought sunflower sea stars close to extinction. But there is hope! Scientists are breeding them in captivity to boost their numbers.

FACT: *Some groups of sea stars have begun growing extra arms. Scientists are studying these creatures to find out why.*

Zombie deer

Name: *wild deer (various species)*

Area of the world: *deer can be found in many parts of the world, but zombie deer have mainly been observed across America*

Habitat: *ranges from savannas to tropical rainforests*

Appearance:

- *red or brown coat*
- *male deer have antlers which they can shed and then regrow; in some species, the females have antlers too*

Deer are famous for their antlers, but did you know that they shed them every year? This yearly cycle begins each spring, when the deer shed their old antlers and then begin to grow new ones. As deer age, the antlers they grow become more complex. Healthy male deer can grow large and impressive antlers.

Did you know that the size of a deer's nose indicates how old they are? In general, the longer a deer's snout, the older they are!

The first zombie deer disease case was discovered over 50 years ago in Colorado, USA. The deer exhibited zombie-like symptoms: they had a vacant stare, drooled, didn't eat and stumbled about in an uncoordinated way. In time, scientists worked out that this was the result of a disease, which became known as zombie deer disease. The official name is chronic wasting disease (CWD) because it affects the deer's brain, so they stop eating and waste away.

FACT: *Despite the name, other creatures have been recorded as having zombie deer disease, including elks and moose.*

Zombie pigeons

Name: pigeon

Area of the world: across the world, but zombie pigeons have been observed in Britain

Habitat: rural and urban habitats

Appearance:
- *feathers range in colour — blue, white, black, grey*
- *short legs*
- *short bills*
- *small heads*

Pigeons are a common sight throughout Britain. They are gentle birds, known for the bobbing movement of their head as they walk. Pigeons have a reputation for scavenging food waste from humans. However, they are intelligent birds that can be tamed and trained for pigeon racing or carrying messages, due to their excellent navigation skills.

The first zombie pigeons were spotted in Jersey (an island between France and England) in 2022. The pigeons had twisted necks and green faces, and they walked around in circles with trembling wings. Newspapers began to report that they were 'zombie pigeons' because the symptoms were so severe. But what was causing this freaky behaviour?

Scientists discovered that a disease (paramyxovirus) had infected the pigeons. The virus spreads easily, and sadly, any pigeons infected die within a few days.

> **FACT:** *There is good news! Pigeons can be vaccinated against this virus, which will slow down the spread of the disease.*

CHAPTER 4
Mind control parasites

Some creatures become zombie-like because of parasites. But what are parasites?

Parasites live on or inside another living thing (which is called the host). Many parasites just live in their host's body, using them for food, shelter or both. However, some parasites seem to take over the mind of their hosts, making them act like zombies.

Let's look at some of these zombie creatures.

Which parasite makes zombie snails?

Type of parasite: parasitic flatworm

Name: green-banded broodsac

Area of the world: many places including Germany, Poland, Russia, UK, Sweden, Norway, Japan

Habitat: marshes and other moist places where the host snails are found

Appearance:
- green bands and brown and black spots in the eyestalks of the host snail

snail infected by green-banded broodsac

Zombie snails start their lives as normal land snails. So, what makes them become zombie snails? Be prepared … the following information is gruesome.

These snails become infected by eating bird poo which has been infected with parasitic worms called green-banded broodsacs. The parasitic worms grow in the snails and take them over, transforming them into zombies!

When snails are infected, their eyestalks become brightly coloured. These wriggly eyestalks look like caterpillars and are irresistible to hungry birds!

When the birds eat the eyestalks, they become infected by the parasitic worms, which breed inside them. Eventually the birds produce infected poo, which other snails eat. And so, the cycle starts all over again.

Incredibly, the parasitic worms control the movement of the infected snails. This means they can ensure that the snails move to places where birds are more likely to notice them!

- Yum! — snail eats infected bird poo
- green-banded broadsacs take over the snail's eyestalks
- Yum! — bird eats the green eyestalks
- bird's poo contains parasitic worms

FACT: Zombie snails move faster than your everyday snails! No one really knows why. It could be that the parasitic worms make the zombie snails move faster so they can be eaten sooner.

Which parasite makes zombie ants?

Type of parasite: **fungus**

Name: zombie ant fungus

Area of the world: mainly tropical forests

an ant infected by zombie ant fungus

Zombie ant fungus takes over carpenter ants and turns them into zombie ants. This fungus starts life as **spores** on a rainforest floor. These spores are sticky and can attach to carpenter ants' bodies. The spores find their way inside the ants and the fungus grows.

The ants begin to behave strangely as the fungus takes control of them. Carpenter ants nest in decaying wood, but zombie ants will leave their nests and colonies. The fungus releases chemicals into their brains which affect the ants' behaviour and make them move to a warm place, under a leaf, near to the ground.

When the ants eventually die, a spore spike pokes out of them. This releases more spores onto the ground below, ready for new unsuspecting ants.

FACT: Carpenter ants have developed their own defence from zombie ant fungus. In heavily infected areas of the rainforest, the ants tend to avoid the forest floor. They therefore avoid the sticky spores lying on the ground.

Which parasite makes zombie cockroaches?

Type of parasite: *wasp*

Name: *emerald cockroach wasp*

Area of the world: *tropical regions of Africa, South Asia, Southeast Asia and the Pacific Islands*

Habitat: *tropical regions, warm climates*

Appearance:
- *metallic blue-green body*
- *females have a stinger; males don't*

an emerald cockroach wasp

In tropical parts of the world, cockroaches could become zombies! This can happen if they're unlucky enough to meet an emerald cockroach wasp. These wasps like to lay their eggs inside cockroaches – and to do that, they paralyse the cockroach and take over its body.

When a female wasp is ready to lay its eggs, it finds a cockroach. Then it stings the cockroach, not once, but twice. Why does it do this?

The wasp needs the cockroach to be still so it can sting in precisely the right place. The first sting paralyses the cockroach's front legs so it can't move.

Then, the wasp stings again, straight into the cockroach's brain. Next, the wasp injects venom into the cockroach and this makes the cockroach change its behaviour.

The cockroach is now unable to escape or move of its own free will. The wasp grabs the cockroach's antennae and pulls it to the nest. It conceals the entrance to the nest with pebbles to block it from predators. Inside the nest, the wasp lays its eggs on the cockroach. The eggs hatch into wasp larvae which feed on the cockroach. Eventually, the cockroach dies, and the larvae make a cocoon inside the dead body. When the wasps leave the cocoon, they fly off to find a mate … and the whole cycle starts again.

FACT: *Cockroaches have bacteria inside them which would be harmful to the wasp larvae. But the larvae have a defence for this. They cover the inside of the cockroach's body with antibiotics, to keep away any infection.*

Which parasite makes zombie spiders?

Type of parasite: wasp

Name: Costa Rican parasitic wasp

Area of the world: Costa Rica

Habitat: heavy vegetation

Appearance:

- wings vary in colour — black, orange with black markings, patterned black and yellow, or translucent
- black head

Costa Rican parasitic wasp infecting a spider

Like the zombified cockroaches, parasitic wasps can take over a specific type of orb-weaver spider and zombify them.

These parasitic wasps are **native** to Costa Rica. The wasps use spiders as hosts for their eggs. A wasp will paralyse a spider with its sting. Once the spider can't move, the wasp puts its eggs inside the spider's body.

Leucauge argyra spider, a type of orb-weaver spider

When the eggs hatch, the larvae then feed on the host spider. When the larvae have grown enough, they release chemicals to control the spider. They make it spin an extra-strong web, strong enough to support cocoons. This is different from any web the spider has spun before. Once the new web is ready, the larvae kill the zombie spider. Then each larva goes into its cocoon to grow, ready to emerge as a wasp.

> **FACT:** *These parasitic wasps play an important role in keeping **ecosystems** in balance in Costa Rica. They control the population of the spiders, preventing them from becoming too dominant.*

Bonus
CLASSIFIED: NEW DISCOVERY

Year of discovery: 2021

Location: Castle Espie, Northern Ireland

Fungus: *Gibellula attenboroughii*

Details: During filming for a BBC documentary, a never-before-seen type of fungus was discovered on a dead cave spider. This new fungus has been named after Sir David Attenborough.

Investigations have discovered the fungus in several caves in Ireland. The infected dead spiders were out in the open, on the roofs of the caves.

A possible explanation is that the fungus takes over the spiders' behaviour, so they move out of dark crevices, making it easier for the fungus to spread its spores. This is a similar process to what happens to the carpenter 'zombie' ants when infected by a fungus.

CHAPTER 5
Ghost creatures

Some creatures get their ghostly names because the way they look and behave reminds us of ghosts.

History of ghosts

Ghosts have appeared in stories for thousands of years. They crop up in different forms, but they always have one thing in common. They represent the spirit of a dead person.

There is evidence that belief in ghosts has been around since ancient times. Lurking in the British Museum's stores, was a forgotten 3,500-year-old clay tablet from the ancient city of Babylon. When the tablet was rediscovered in 2021, experts studied it, and they realised that it might include the world's earliest drawing of a ghost!

After careful investigation, the experts worked out that the tablet shows a ghost ritual. People in ancient Babylon carried out this ritual in order to allow ghosts to pass over to the underworld. This confirms that the Babylonians of over 3,000 years ago believed in ghosts.

In ancient Greek mythology, when somebody died, their spirit was guided to the underworld. Hades was the god of the underworld and, in the stories, there were also two goddesses whose roles were to oversee the spirits of the restless dead. In other words – ghosts!

About 2,000 years ago, an author called Pliny the Younger wrote about hearing a ghost rattling chains in a house in Athens, Greece.

In fact, ghosts can be found in folklore from across the globe, including ancient cultures in China, Egypt and India.

Today, when we think of ghosts, we might imagine them in different ways. Sometimes as strange noises, such as chains rattling, or objects moving on their own. Other times as the form of a person, wearing historical clothes from the time when they died.

Another common way to imagine ghosts is to think of them floating about under a white sheet (or a shroud). This is probably because up until about 100 years ago, dead people were wrapped in a white burial shroud.

This image of ghosts as floating white sheets has inspired people to give some creatures a ghostly nickname!

Ghost owls

Name: barn owl

Nickname: ghost owl

Area of the world: every continent except Antarctica

Habitat: holes in trees, barns, outbuildings

Appearance:
- weighs as much as a grapefruit
- knee-height to an adult human
- pale colour
- heart-shaped face

Barn owls are nocturnal. When they fly, they look like ghosts as they swoop silently overhead, due to their white face, pale wings and dark eyes. It's no wonder they got the nickname 'ghost owl'. Even though their wings are silent in flight, barn owls are well known for their screeching call. However, this isn't the only sound they make – they also hiss and yap. So, not so silent, after all!

Barn owls are excellent hunters. They mostly prey on voles and field mice, but also hunt snakes, other reptiles and fish. Barn owls have excellent hearing, so they can accurately locate their prey and catch it easily. In fact, scientists think they have better hearing than any other bird.

Barn owls also have brilliant night vision, which helps them hunt in the dark. What's more, they can rotate their heads almost three-quarters of the way around. This increases their range of vision and allows them to see behind them.

Their silent flight means they can swoop down and grab their prey in their talons without warning. They swallow their meals whole, and then regurgitate any inedible parts, like fur and bone, into what is called owl pellets.

To go with their spooky 'ghost owl' nickname, there are plenty of superstitions about barn owls. They are associated with banshees, a type of spirit from Irish folklore which were said to appear when a family member was close to death. In some parts of the world, including Mexico, Malaysia and parts of Africa and India, barn owls are seen as a bad omen.

Barn owls have earned themselves many different nicknames. Here are some of the other names barn owls have been given:

- hobgoblin owl
- demon owl
- death owl
- corpse bird.

FACT: The cycle of the moon changes the amount of light at night. A new moon means the night is darker, making it easier for barn owls to hunt their prey without being detected. When it's a full moon, you might think the brightness of the moon would be a disadvantage for barn owls, as it makes it easier for them to be seen. However, this also works to the owls' advantage, as it's also easier for them to see their prey. What's more, the moonlight reflects off the barn owls' feathers and stops prey such as rodents in their tracks! This makes it much easier for the barn owls to catch their prey.

Ghost moths

Name: ghost moth

Area of the world: most of Europe

Habitat: grassy areas

Appearance:

- males are white

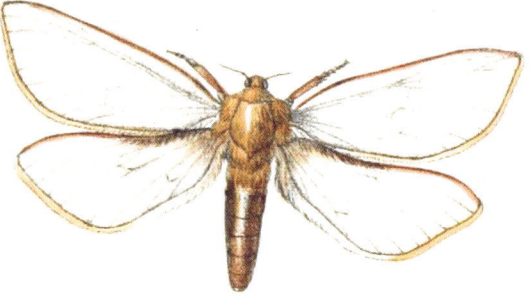

- females have a gold pattern

Ghost moths are common in most of Europe, but how did they get their name? There are a few reasons that could explain this, so let's dig a little deeper!

The males of the species have white wings, and as we often think of ghosts as white, this seems a likely explanation for their name. However, there could be another reason too. When it is time to attract a mate, the male ghost moths have a specific hovering pattern. They gather together in a group called a lek and perform a dance, hovering up and down. At the same time, they give off a stinky smell. This hovering dance is almost ghostlike in movement!

Once they've mated, the female ghost moths lay their eggs in the soil. These hatch into caterpillars and it can then take two years or more for them to develop into moths. The caterpillars feed on plant roots, before creating a cocoon, and finally hatching out as adult ghost moths. Ghost moths are unable to feed as they have no working mouth parts. This means their whole purpose, once they've developed into moths, is to mate and produce eggs.

FACT: *Moths hold a special place in folklore. They are often seen as messengers of the dead or the soul of a dead person. Maybe this is another reason these moths have been called ghost moths?*

Bonus
More Creepy Creatures

Yeti crabs
(also known as yeti lobsters)

In 2005, scientists discovered a new type of crab. They were named 'yeti crab' because they are pale and hairy, just like a **yeti**!

Goliath birdeaters

Goliath birdeater spiders are the largest of all tarantulas. Despite their name, they don't often eat birds. Insects make up most of their diet. They pounce on their prey and pierce their skin using their fangs, before injecting toxins into them. The spiders then suck out the prey's insides!

Death's-head hawk moths

These moths' famous skull-shaped markings explain how they got their name. They were once thought of as a bad omen.

CHAPTER 6
Newly discovered ghost creatures

Did you know that around 18,000 new species of plants and animals are discovered every year? A lot of these new discoveries are tiny creatures, such as insects, but scientists and explorers also often find larger animals and plants that have never been seen before. Areas of the world that are harder to visit are often the best places for new discoveries – like dense rainforests, underground habitats or the deep sea.

Everyone loves a ghost story, so it's no wonder that newly discovered species are sometimes given ghostly names!

Ghost octopuses

Name: ghost octopus

Area of the world: off the coast of Hawaii

Habitat: Pacific Ocean, 4,000 metres deep

Appearance:
- body is jellylike
- white in colour
- eight short arms
- no fins

Ghost octopuses lack special cells called pigment cells, which give other creatures their colour. They're therefore very pale and it's this pale appearance which inspired the name ghost octopus.

Ghost octopuses are a recent discovery. In 2016, a submarine robot called *Deep Discoverer* captured a ghost octopus on video! The octopus was nicknamed 'Casper' after the cartoon ghost.

All newly discovered creatures get a special scientific name. However, at the time of writing this book, ghost octopuses haven't yet received theirs. This is because no specimens have been collected yet and all that we know about these octopuses is from the video footage.

Ghost octopuses are well adapted to living deep in the ocean, where it is almost completely dark and there is little food. Their body is jellylike and has very few muscles, which means they require less energy to survive and therefore need less food than most animals.

FACT: *Mother ghost octopuses will die for their young. They lay about 30 eggs on dead sponges and wrap themselves around the eggs to keep them safe. They wait for the eggs to hatch, without any food. They will wait for years and years! Finally, the eggs hatch and the mothers wane away, eventually dying.*

Ghost slugs

Name: ghost slug

Area of the world: mainly South Wales, also sightings in England and other parts of Wales, also Ukraine

Habitat: underground; mountain forests in Ukraine

Appearance:
- *white/pale grey body*
- *sharp teeth*
- *no eyes*
- *smaller than a finger in length*

Before 2006, ghost slugs were completely unknown to scientists. One of the reasons we don't know much about them is because they live up to one metre underground and rarely come to the surface. They were first recorded in South Wales, UK, but scientists don't think they are native to the UK. Scientists have since recorded the slugs in mountain forests in Ukraine and think they probably originate from there.

Most slugs have their breathing hole near the front of their body, but ghost slugs have the breathing hole at the back. Unlike many other slugs, ghost slugs are carnivores; they hunt for earthworms during the night, feeding on them with their blade-like teeth, and suck them up like spaghetti!

FACT: We don't know much about ghost slugs. However, due to their pale colour and lack of eyes, it is likely they originated in caves. Most caves are in complete darkness so creatures that live their whole lives there don't need the ability to see. As sunlight doesn't reach inside caves, the creatures don't need dark pigments in their skin to protect against the sun, so they are pale.

Ghost spiders

Name: ghost spider

Area of the world: across the world

Habitat: often found near water

Appearance:
- eight eyes
- eight legs
- pale brown body

There are over 500 different species of ghost spider around the world, and most of them have been known about for many years. They're called ghost spiders because they are extremely quick and difficult to see. They are mainly nocturnal, hunting at night, and in the daytime, they spin silk sacs on plants or under rocks and hide behind the sacs.

In 2023, scientists identified six new species of ghost spider in South America. They were looking through records of spiders that had previously been observed, and realised that some of them belonged to the ghost spider family. Nobody had realised that when the spiders were first seen.

FACT: *There are 50,000 known species of spiders that live in habitats all across the world. Scientists are often discovering new ones, so it is likely that there are more undiscovered species of ghost spiders out there!*

Ghost snakes

Name: *ghost snake*

Area of the world: *Madagascar*

Habitat: *mainly found in rock formations*

Appearance:
- *pale grey colour*
- *black and white spots*
- *cat-like eyes*
- *larger teeth at the back of the mouth*

In 2016, a team of researchers were hiking in Madagascar and discovered a new species of snake in a lime rock formation – the ghost snake.

Ghost snakes are a type of cat-eyed snake. These get their name because the pupils in their eyes are vertical slits like a cat's pupils.

Ghost snakes are nocturnal.

'Ghost snake' is a suitable name because the snakes avoided discovery, even though researchers had **surveyed** their habitat many times before.

The scientific name of the snakes reflects their ghostly grey colour and includes 'lolo', which is a word for 'ghost' in Madagascar.

There haven't been many sightings of ghost snakes, and this may be due to their habitat. As they are nocturnal, they will be most active in the night when it is dark. Scientists believe they live in rock formations, which are difficult for humans to navigate, especially in darkness.

> **FACT:** Did you know that snakes use their tongue to help them smell?
>
> They flick their tongue to gather smelly particles in the air. Then they pull it back to a special part of the mouth that helps them work out what the smells are.

New species

As ghost octopuses, ghost slugs, ghost spiders and ghost snakes are only recent discoveries, there is still a lot we don't know about them.

For any newly discovered species, it is important that researchers carry on finding out about these creatures, so we can understand and protect them from any potential dangers, such as habitat loss.

Who knows what other creepy creatures scientists might discover in the future?

Bonus
CREATURES OF THE DEEP

There are some very creepy creatures lurking in the DEEPEST depths of our oceans.

Fangtooth fish

These are small, bony fish, with humongous jaws and large, sharp teeth.

Black seadevil anglerfish

These fish have huge jaws and sharp fangs. They have **lures** that emit light to attract their prey. They look terrifying – but fear not! They are only as big as your hand.

Goblin sharks

Goblin sharks are named after a type of Japanese goblin called a Tengu which has a pointed nose. They can thrust their jaws forwards out of their mouth to catch their prey.

Ghost shrimps

Ghost shrimps have a threadlike, thin body, which is almost transparent. When they hide among plants, they are almost invisible.

Glossary

clotting when blood changes from a liquid into a solid

deciduous a tree which loses its leaves in autumn

ecosystems the living things in an area and how they affect that environment and each other

evolution the way living things change over time

filaments thin threads

fungus a group of living things that behave like plants but can't make their own food so feed off other living things

immortal living forever

kelp forests underwater areas with lots of large brown seaweed

larvae young insects that haven't developed adult features yet

lures things that are used to attract other animals so they can be caught

mucus a slimy liquid

native plants and animals that are naturally from a place

nocturnal normally being active and awake at night

parasites animals or plants which live on, or inside, another animal or plant and cause harm to it

regurgitate bring swallowed food back up

rocky reefs groups of rocks that are always or sometimes under water

spores cells that can develop into new living things

surveyed measured and recorded details

yeti a mythical snow monster

About the author

What made you want to be an author?

I've always enjoyed writing ever since I was a child and, throughout my life, it's something that I've kept coming back to. When I trained as a teacher and became a mum, I was plunged into a world of children's books and fell in love with them. It was then that I decided to write books for children. There's something special about writing books and being able to share my ideas with the future generation.

Emily Ann Davison

What's the best part of being an author?

There are so many parts that I enjoy – coming up with ideas, holding a copy of my book for the first time and meeting the children who I write the books for! For this book, I loved researching the creatures and finding out lots of fascinating facts.

How did you come up with the idea for this book?

Years ago, I stumbled across a fact about vampire bats and it inspired me to find out about other creepy creatures. I liked the idea of mashing up facts about the real creatures in our world with the not-so-real creepy creatures from folklore.

What was the best thing you learnt while writing this?

That penguins shoot poo at vampire bats! As a child, penguins were my favourite animals and I collected anything to do with them. Now I'm grown up, I still find them fascinating and quite comical! I love that Humboldt penguins won't take any nonsense from vampire bats and will shoo them away, by any means necessary, even if that means squirting poo at them.

Do you have a favourite creepy creature?

The ghost octopus is my favourite creepy creature in this book, although it isn't all that creepy (apart from its name). It looks so cute and I find it fascinating that it has only been recently discovered and doesn't even have a scientific name yet!

What do you hope readers get from this book?

I hope this book will ignite a passion and fascination for the world we live in, and that these feelings will prompt readers to care for the world throughout their lives.

What would you like to write about next?

Writing this book has really inspired me. There are two things included in it which I'd love to find out more about – the creatures which are living fossils, such as vampire squids, who have hardly changed over millions of years and secondly, the creatures that have only recently been discovered. I'd love to write more about both types.

Book chat

What did you think this book would be about? Were you right?

Have you ever seen any of these creatures?

Which creature would you most like to see and why?

Which creature do you not want to see and why?

Which animal do you think has the best name?

If you had to think of a new title for this book, what would it be?

What's your favourite picture in the book?

If you could ask the author anything, what would you ask?

Who would you recommend this book to and why?

Do you have a favourite photograph in this book?

If you had to give this book a three-word review, what would you say?

Could you give the author a piece of advice to make the book even better?

What was the most interesting fact you learnt in this book?

What do you think about the names that scientists give animals?

If you had to name a new species, how would you do it?

Would you like to learn more about any of the creatures in this book?

Book challenge:

Draw your own creepy creature and give it a creepy name. Where does it live and what does it eat?

Published by Collins
An imprint of HarperCollins*Publishers*

The News Building
1 London Bridge Street
London
SE1 9GF
UK

Macken House
39/40 Mayor Street Upper
Dublin 1
D01 C9W8
Ireland

Emily Ann Davison asserts her moral right to be identified as the author of this work.

Text © Emily Ann Davison 2025
Design and illustrations ©
HarperCollins*Publishers* Limited 2025

Maps © Collins Bartholomew 2025

10 9 8 7 6 5 4 3 2 1

ISBN 978-0-00-876785-3

All rights reserved. No part of this publication may be reproduced, stored in a retrieval system, or transmitted in any form by any means, electronic, mechanical, photocopying, recording or otherwise, without the prior written permission of the Publisher or a licence permitting restricted copying in the United Kingdom issued by the Copyright Licensing Agency Ltd, 5th Floor, Shackleton House, 4 Battle Bridge Lane, London SE1 2HX.

Without limiting the exclusive rights of any author, contributor or the publisher of this publication, any unauthorised use of this publication to train generative artificial intelligence (AI) technologies is expressly prohibited. HarperCollins also exercise their rights under Article 4(3) of the Digital Single Market Directive 2019/790 and expressly reserve this publication from the text and data mining exception.

British Library Cataloguing-in-Publication Data A catalogue record for this publication is available from the British Library.

Download the teaching notes and word cards to accompany this book at:
http://littlewandle.org.uk/signupfluency/

Get the latest Collins Big Cat news at
collins.co.uk/collinsbigcat

Author: Emily Ann Davison
Publisher: Laura White
Commissioning editor and product manager: Caroline Green
Series editor: Charlotte Raby
Development editor: Catherine Baker
Project manager: Emily Hooton
Copyeditor: Sally Byford
Proofreader: Catherine Dakin
Cover designer: Sarah Finan
Typesetter: 2Hoots Publishing Services Ltd
Production controller: Katharine Willard

Printed in the UK.

This book contains FSC™ certified paper and other controlled sources to ensure responsible forest management.

For more information visit: www.harpercollins.co.uk/green

Made with responsibly sourced paper and vegetable ink

Scan to see how we are reducing our environmental impact.

Acknowledgements
The publishers gratefully acknowledge the permission granted to reproduce the copyright material in this book. Every effort has been made to trace copyright holders and to obtain their permission for the use of copyright material. The publishers will gladly receive any information enabling them to rectify any error or omission at the first opportunity.

Front cover t, p6, p22 Nathapol Kongseang/Shutterstock, bl, Tobias Hauke/Shutterstock, br, p91 Sterling E/Shutterstock, p8 SuperStock/Alamy, p10 booksR/Alamy, p12 The History Collection Alamy, p15 Solvin Zankl/Alamy, p16 wikimedia commons, p17 James Armstrong/Alamy, p20 Niday Picture Library/Alamy, p21 warmcolors/Getty Images, p25 Steve Lillie/Alamy, p26 The History Collection/Alamy, p27 Nature Picture Library/Alamy, p28 Chronicle/Alamy, p30 Joel Sartore/Photo Ark/Nature Picture Library, p31 Royal Geographical Society/Getty Images, p32 Chroma Collection/Alamy, p33 Pete Oxford/Nature Picture Library p36 Krys Bailey/Alamy, p39 PetaPix/Alamy, p40, 54 Suriya Siritam/Alamy, p41 Suriya Siritam/Alamy, p43 Neil Gilham/ Getty Images, p45 All Canada Photos/Alamy, p47 Star Tribune/ Getty Images, p48 pumkinpie/Alamy, p56 Frank Hecker/Alamy, p58r BIOSPHOTO/Alamy, p59 Kevin Wells/Alamy, p62 Dorling Kindersley ltd/Alamy, p63 FLPA/Alamy, p65 Creative Commons Attribution-Share Alike License 3.0 (Unported) (CC BY-SA), p66 piemags/nature/Alamy, p69 Dr Harry Evans/CABI, p70, 80, 83, 86 Reading Room 2020/Alamy, p72 The British Museum/Trustees of the British Museum, p75 Farida Biktimirova/Alamy, p79 David Tipling Photo Library/Alamy, p81l Alex Hyde/Nature Picture Library, p84 Fifis Alexis, Ifremer (2005), https://image.ifremer.fr/ data/00569/68091/, p85t Nature Picture Library/Alamy, p88, 100 Science History Images/Alamy, p89 Science History Images/Alamy p93, 100tr Rachel Kolokoff Hopper/Alamy, p94, 100br Stefan Sollfors/Alamy, p97, 100bl Sara Ruane/Negaunee Integrative Research Center Field Museum of Natural History, p102 Solvin Zankl/Nature Picture Library, p103t & back cover Kelvin Aitken/ VWPics/Alamy, p103c Animal Stock/Alamy, p103b Blue Planet Archive LLC/Alamy, back cover t Nature Photographers Ltd/Alamy All other photos Shutterstock.